My DOG'S Journal

PUPPY MILESTONES...
TRAINING TACTICS... DOGGY IQ AND MORE

Illustrated by GEMMA CORRELL

MICHAEL POWELL

spruce

An Hachette UK Company
www.hachette.co.uk

First published in Great Britain in 2013 by Spruce
A division of Octopus Publishing Group Ltd
Endeavour House, 189 Shaftesbury Avenue,
London, WC2H 8JY
www.octopusbooks.co.uk
www.octopusbooksusa.com

Distributed in the US by Hachette Book Group USA
237 Park Avenue, New York, NY 10017, USA

Distributed in Canada by Canadian Manda Group
165 Dufferin Street, Toronto, Ontario, Canada M6K 3H6

ISBN 978 1 84601 475 8

Printed and bound in China

10 9 8 7 6 5 4 3 2 1
CONSULTANT PUBLISHER Sarah Ford
EDITOR Ellie Smith
COPY-EDITOR Jo Richardson
DESIGN Eoghan O'Brien & Clare Barber
ILLUSTRATOR Gemma Correll
ASSISTANT PRODUCTION MANAGER Lucy Carter

Contents

Congratulations!

You are about to become a dog owner and that dog is me! It's lots of fun but it's also a huge commitment, and it has nothing to do with my size or breed. All dogs are demanding of your time, and need strong leadership, clear rules and limits, and plenty of exercise.

Use this journal to learn more about me, to record my personal details, some of the things I do, as well as our shared memories together. Don't forget to stick in lots of cute photos, too.

Ten things you should know about me:

1. I am a D-O-G, so please treat me like one. I am not a human with four legs, a bigger nose, and more hair!
2. I need your attention, protection, and care.
3. Learn to speak and understand my language. Here's a clue: it's not English!
4. You are the pack leader. I don't want that responsibility. I want an easy life!
5. Show me how to behave by rewarding good conduct and ignoring or correcting bad conduct, but never use physical punishment.
6. Be patient! I'm not as smart as you.
7. Always be consistent; and that goes for everyone in the household.
8. Mixed messages and inconsistency make me anxious.
9. Never stop learning about me and my needs!
10. Dogs get bored, too.

Canine charter

Before you consider bringing me home to chew on your slippers, read the small print carefully and then sign on the dotted line!

We the undersigned promise to show

.... [my name]

love and strong leadership and make it easy for him/her to succeed and be happy. We will be consistent and try to remain calm and stable at all times. We understand that we are entering into a lifelong commitment, so under no circumstances will he/she have to join the millions of wonderful dogs that end up in shelters every year. We will not put off taking him/her to the vet, and will never, ever leave him/her in a parked car, even if there is a window open; not even for a second.

Signed ....

Date ....

Pooch profile

Name
....

Nickname
....

Breed
....

Date of birth
....

Place of birth
....

Age on arrival at home
....

Eyes
....

Fur and markings
....

Height and weight
....

ID chip/ collar
....

I may be small but I've got kennel-loads of personality. Now, it's time to do some canine homework: Google my breed (or breeds if I'm mixed-breed) and see the traits that apply to me.

....

....

....

Hi! My name is...

....

My age is...   /
....
            months/years old
My breed is...

....

Where I came from

Place photograph here
of me
before I arrived

Here's me at my
other home

Name of previous owner/breeder/pet shop
....

....

My new home

Here I am with my new family. Date:
....

Place passport size
photograph here

There are   people in my new home.

Their names are
....

There are   pets in my house (including me).

Their names are
....

My bed is in the
....

What I did on my first day
....

....

....

My first week

If I am to settle in quickly and feel totally at home, then my first few days are really important in setting up good habits and routines. Establish the house rules now and stick to them (see pages 60–61).

• Bring me home on a Friday, so we can have the whole weekend together. If I am a puppy I will need almost constant supervision during my first 24 hours. Also, don't invite everyone and his dog around to see me; keep things low-key and only expose me to close family members at first. I need to feel comfortable with my new pack (that's you).

• Don't handle me too much: I know I'm cute, but it can stress me out at first until I get to know you better. Encourage me to follow you rather than lift and carry me from place to place.

• Don't let me wander all over the house. Let me stay in the room with you, so you can keep me out of trouble. Choose where you want me to relieve myself, and start taking me to that spot right now. Preventing problems is better than allowing me to get into difficulties.

Things I like about my new home

....

....

....

Things I find scary

....

....

....

....

Place photograph here

Here's me on my first day with my new pack!

CHAPTER 1

All about ME

The more you can learn about my character and those of my breed(s), the easier it will be for you to take care of me so that we can live in blissful harmony together (until the next time I dig up the yard). You should never stop learning about dogs, because a well-informed dog owner is a better dog owner, and an expert is a joy to be around. If you want to be really popular with dogs, keep learning.

My breed and me

Dogs have been bred for thousands of years. Today there are more than 350 breeds, and each one has a distinct temperament, characteristics, and needs. For example, some need much more exercise than others, or are nervous or prone to barking at mail carriers! It's your job to bone up on my breed (did you see what I did there?) so that you have a general idea of the sort of traits that I may display. Contact a breed society for breed-specific information, however, don't forget that I'm an individual too, and that most of my personality is formed from birth to one year of age (although it actually is possible to teach old dogs new tricks).

I am a working/hound/sporting/
toy/non-sporting/terrier/herding dog,
which means...

....

....

....

My breed history can be traced back to
....

We were bred to
....

We are good at
....

We are bad at
....

We are prone to
....

Build
....

Weight .... lb/kg

Height .... inches/cm

Coat
....

Head
....

Teeth
....

Eyes
....

Ears
....

Tail
....

Legs
....

Feet
....

Life span
....

Other breed-specific features include
....

....

....

My Personality

How much exercise I need as a puppy
....

....

How much exercise I need as an adult
....

....

Energy levels
....

....

Intelligence
....

....

Response to training
....

....

Confidence/nervousness
....

....

How I am with other dogs

....

....

How I am with children

....

....

Wanderlust!

....

....

Cat chasing

....

....

Keep off my patch!

....

....

What I need to eat

....

....

Other things my breed needs

....

....

....

Personality test

From fit-in-the-palm-of-your-hand Chihuahuas to beefy Newfoundlands, we dogs have some really strong drives, depending on our breed and individual personality.

ANSWER ALL OF THE FORTY QUESTIONS: there are ten in each section. Check the box for a YES, otherwise leave it blank. The sections with the most checkmarks show whether I am a Hunter, Teammate, Fighter, or a Scaredy-cat!

HUNTER Do I?

- ☐ Sniff the ground or air lots?
- ☐ Chase things (cats, rabbits, balls, joggers, bicycles, cars, etc.)?
- ☐ Have a high-pitched bark when excited?
- ☐ Pounce on toys or shake them to death?
- ☐ Steal food when you're not looking?
- ☐ Tear up soft things?
- ☐ Wolf down my food?
- ☐ Like carrying stuff?
- ☐ Love digging holes?
- ☐ Bury stuff?

TEAMMATE Do I?

- ☐ Make friends with other dogs?
- ☐ Enjoy playing lots with you and/or other dogs?
- ☐ Make friends with people easily?
- ☐ Bark or go wee when left alone?
- ☐ Like being hugged and stroked?
- ☐ Like being groomed?
- ☐ Follow you around?
- ☐ Jump up to say hello?
- ☐ Make frequent eye contact with you?
- ☐ Respond to verbal praise?

FIGHTER Do I?

- ☐ Check out strange sounds or objects?
- ☐ Enjoy new situations?
- ☐ Play tug-of-war games to win?
- ☐ Bark or growl with a deep voice?
- ☐ Guard my territory, you, or my food or toys?
- ☐ Dislike being petted?
- ☐ Dislike being groomed?
- ☐ Bully other dogs?
- ☐ Get picked on by older dogs?
- ☐ Like to fight with other dogs?

SCAREDY-CAT Do I?

- ☐ Run away from new situations?
- ☐ Hide behind you when feeling insecure?
- ☐ Crawl on my belly or turn upside-down when scolded?
- ☐ Bite when cornered?
- ☐ Avoid direct distractions?
- ☐ Tremble, whine, or wee when unsure?
- ☐ Avoid coming close when you call?
- ☐ Cringe when a stranger stands over me?
- ☐ Try to escape when being examined?
- ☐ Wee during a greeting

HUNTER I am dominant and full of energy. I get excited by anything that moves, new smells and sounds, and I am easily distracted. I can be harder to train than Teammates, unless you show me that you are the top dog.

TEAMMATE I am super-friendly and eager to please and quite calm and laidback, and I love close company. Training should be quite easy, as long as you give me clear and consistent instructions and plenty of praise.

FIGHTER I am tough and sometimes even aggressive. It is vital that you show me that you are the boss otherwise I will end up running the household.

SCAREDY-CAT I need lots of reassurance, especially in unfamiliar situations and surroundings. Don't back down: help me to face my fears and play with me lots, and my confidence will grow.

My family tree

Discovering my family tree is fun and can also provide insight into my personality and possible health issues. Before getting a puppy, you should already have a good idea about the temperament of my parents; if not, find out as much as you can and write it down here. If you got me from a dog shelter, then it might be harder to trace my lineage, but not impossible. Who knows, if you go back far enough you may discover I have ancestors with blue blood (go back 15,000 years and I'm a wolf)!

If you are really stuck (or I'm a mixed-breed) you can find out my genetic information from a Beltsville-based company called MetaMorphix Inc., which offers a Canine Heritage Breed Test kit with a simple swab test. Rub the big Q-tip inside my cheek, pop it in the mail, and after six weeks they will get back to you with the results.

MY DNA TEST RESULTS

....

....

....

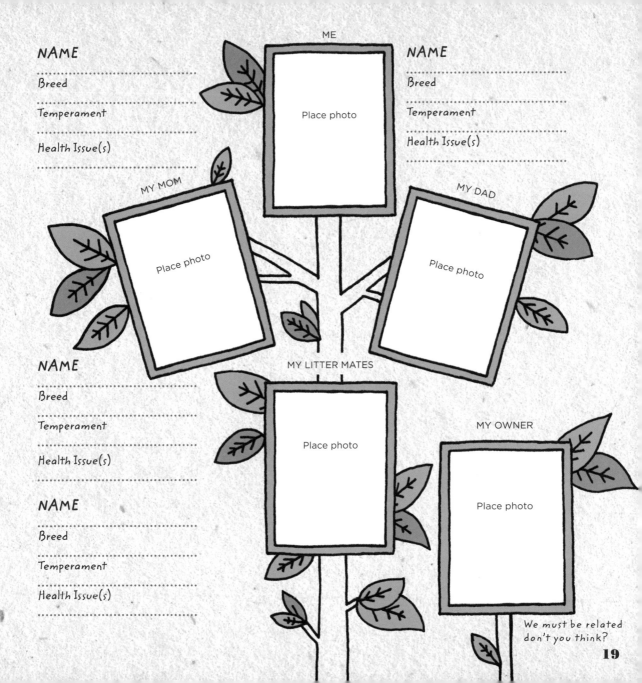

NAME
....

Breed
....

Temperament
....

Health Issue(s)
....

NAME
....

Breed
....

Temperament
....

Health Issue(s)
....

ME

Place photo

NAME
....

Breed
....

Temperament
....

Health Issue(s)
....

MY MOM

Place photo

MY DAD

Place photo

NAME
....

Breed
....

Temperament
....

Health Issue(s)
....

MY LITTER MATES

Place photo

MY OWNER

Place photo

We must be related don't you think?

19

Things I Like

I may not know how to open the refrigerator (yet), but I know what I like...

....

....

My favorite foods/treats

....

Walks

....

Games

....

Toys (that's me with my favorite toy)

....

Tricks

....

Music

....

Things I Dislike

Yucky food

....

....

Noises

....

....

Other dogs

....

....

These things scare me

....

....

These things make me bark

....

....

Place passport size
photograph here

21

My Doggy IQ

I'm so bright I should be teaching you to fetch sticks, but how do you know unless you test me, right? Come on, you humans just love testing stuff, so try these five easy ones on me. They measure my adaptive intelligence (that's the ability to solve problems, understand language, and learn social cues, in case you didn't know. I told you I was smart!).

TEST 1 Get my full attention by allowing me to sniff a doggy treat, then hide it underneath an empty can about three feet away from me. See what I do next, and use a stopwatch to time me. My score .... /20.

TEST 2 Repeat test 1, only this time cover the treat with a towel. The same scoring applies. My score .... /20.

TEST 3 Get a big dry towel. Let me sniff it (so it doesn't scare me). Now throw it over my head so that it covers my head and shoulders. How long does it take me to escape? My score .... /20.

Scoring
If I get the food/escape:

Within five seconds	20 points
Within 15 seconds	16 points
Within 30 seconds	12 points
Under a minute	8 points
More than a minute	4 points

TEST 4 Can I recognize a smile? Sit about six feet away from me and wait for me to look at you. Stare at me for about three seconds and then give me your best cheesy grin. My score .... /20.

Scoring

If I come bounding over to you with tail wagging, award me 20 points; if I come slowly or some of the way, 16 points; if I stand up but stay put, 12 points; walk away, 4 points; ignore you, 4 points.

TEST 5 When I am lying down, settled, call "Dumbledore" using the same tone as if you were calling my name. If I don't come, call "Slitherin." If I still don't come, call my name.

Scoring

If I only come after you call my name, 20 points; if I come after you call my name a second time, 16 points; If I prick up my ears, lift my head and look like I want to come, 12 points; if I come after "Slitherin," 8 points; if I don't come at all, 4 points.

My JQ

Add all my scores together .... /100 = ... %

....

Over 80%	I am a canine Einstein.
60–79%	I'm smarter than your average feline!
20–59%	I'm not the smoothest dog bone in the box, but I'm still cute.
Below 20%	I'm so dumb I sit on the TV and watch the couch.

Place photograph here

Here's me looking intelligent!

Who are you
calling a nerd?

CHAPTER 2

GOOD
health

Doggie health is made up of several essential
ingredients: good food, regular exercise,
attention and playtime, pest control, grooming,
and don't forget, spaying and neutering.
If you make my health your priority when I'm
a puppy,I'll have less risk of any yucky
health problems in the future.

Signs I'm healthy

Immune system

Although the immune system is invisible (because it's inside my body), there are several external signs that it is strong.

- [ ] Glossy and soft coat
- [ ] I have lots of energy
- [ ] My eyes are clear and bright
- [ ] Nose is cold and moist
- [ ] My wee is clear yellow
- [ ] Alert posture
- [ ] Strong muscles
- [ ] Supple skin
- [ ] Good lung capacity
- [ ] Stools brown and firm

Body condition

- [ ] Well-proportioned figure
- [ ] A waist is visible behind my ribs when viewed from above
- [ ] Skin is flexible and smooth
- [ ] I'm parasite free (fleas, ticks, lice)
- [ ] No small black specs in fur (a sign of fleas)
- [ ] No scabs, growths, white flakes, or red areas
- [ ] Skin inside my ears is light pink and clean
- [ ] I don't scratch my ears or shake my head frequently
- [ ] You can feel my ribs without too much padding

Teeth and gums

- [ ] My breath doesn't smell
- [ ] Teeth are plaque free
- [ ] Gums are firm and pink, black, or spotted (like my skin)
- [ ] My normal body temperature is between 100.9°F (38.3°C) and 102.6°F (39.2°C), but you'll need a rectal thermometer to measure it. Let's agree to skip that one until I'm sick shall we?

Signs I'm unwell

Don't take any chances. Call the vet if I develop any of the symptoms listed below, or if you suspect I'm unwell.

- [ ] Vomiting that doesn't stop after a couple of hours
- [ ] Diarrhea or lots and lots of weeing that lasts for longer than 12 hours
- [ ] Fainting, collapse, or seizure
- [ ] Body temperature below 100.9°F (38.3°C) or above 102.6°F (39.2°C)
- [ ] Loss of balance, staggering, or falling
- [ ] Enlarged or tender abdomen
- [ ] Persistent cough or sneeze
- [ ] Any eye injury
- [ ] Constipation or straining to wee
- [ ] Difficulty breathing or prolonged panting
- [ ] Dramatic increase in appetite for 24 hours or more
- [ ] Loss of appetite for 24 hours or more
- [ ] Excessive drinking
- [ ] Excessive sleeping or unusual lack of activity
- [ ] Lack of energy
- [ ] Limping, holding, or protecting part of my body
- [ ] Persistent scratching at eyes or ears
- [ ] Prolonged excessive restlessness
- [ ] Runny eyes or nose
- [ ] Shivering
- [ ] Suspected breathing obstruction
- [ ] Swelling or rashes
- [ ] Thick discharge from eyes, ears, nose, or broken skin
- [ ] Weight loss
- [ ] Whining for no apparent reason

Don't ignore the signs of illness in the hope that they will go away so you can save yourself a vet's bill.

Growth/weight chart

Feeding and weight

Canine obesity is a growing problem. Studies show that nearly half of dogs in the West are overweight, but the causes are very simple: too much food and too little exercise.

Good nutrition and exercise are vital to keep me healthy. Poor diet and obesity could cause a host of nasty health problems, such as skin problems, arthritis, diabetes, and diseases of the heart, lungs, liver, and kidneys.

Some breeds need more exercise than others. Make sure you know how much I need; however, don't overdo it when I'm a puppy, as too much exercise before my bones have fully developed will lead to joint problems in later life. Check with your vet if you are unsure.

Here's how to tell whether I am a healthy weight. Ideally...
- ☐ My ribs should be easy to feel and if you pinch my skin there should be little flesh between your fingers.
- ☐ When viewed from above my waist should be clearly visible.
- ☐ My belly should be tucked up when viewed from the side.

Weight record

Use this chart to monitor my weight during my lifetime.

								17
								16
								15
								14
								13
								12
								11
								10
								9 YEARS
								8
								7
								6
								5
								4
								3
								2
								1
								9
								6 MONTHS
								3
35/16	31/14	26/12	22/10	18/8	13/6	9/4	5/2	Small
88/40	77/35	66/30	55/25	44/20	33/15	22/10	11/5	Medium
176/80	154/70	132/60	110/50	88/40	66/30	44/20	22/10	Large

LB/KG

My health risks/ problems

HEALTH RISKS or problems commonly found in my breed include

....

....

....

....

MY MEDICAL HISTORY

Date
....

Date
....

Date
....

Date
....

Notes

....
....
....
....
....
....
....
....
....
....
....
....
....
....
....
....
....
....

Visits to the vet

Name of vet
....

Address
....
....
....

Telephone
....

Emergency telephone
....

Opening times
....
....

Date of first vaccination
....

Date of first booster
....

Yearly booster and health check due (month)
....
....
....
....

Why I need vaccinating

Why vaccinations are important

All dogs should be protected by vaccination. Puppies are at great risk from a wide range of infectious diseases that can cause permanent health damage and even death, so they should only mix with other dogs after being fully vaccinated.

Vaccination trains the immune system to react to small doses of a disease, so that it can fight the disease effectively when it comes into contact with it again.

The first one is usually given in two doses at six to eight weeks and about one month later. After that an annual booster injection maintains immunity. Vaccination protects me from these nasties:

PARVOVIRUS An aggressive and potentially fatal disease that attacks the immune system causing vomiting and blood-stained diarrhea.

DISTEMPER A potentially fatal viral infection of the gut, lungs, and nervous system; symptoms include pus-filled runny nose and eyes, and sometimes fits.

INFECTIOUS CANINE HEPATITIS This virus attacks the liver, lungs, kidneys, and eyes and is often fatal.

INFECTIOUS BRONCHITIS One of the more serious strains of kennel cough, this highly infectious upper-respiratory-tract infection causes a harsh hacking cough.

PARAINFLUENZA A milder respiratory disease that causes sneezing, coughing, and runny eyes.

LEPTOSPIROSIS A bacterial infection that can cause lifelong liver and kidney damage and even death.

Year _____ health check

Your dog has been vaccinated against

- ☐ Distemper
- ☐ Hepatitis
- ☐ Leptospirosis
- ☐ Parvovirus
- ☐ Parainfluenza
- ☐ Infectious Bronchitis
- ☐ Rabies
- ☐ Other

VACCINATION BOOSTER

Vaccine/Batch No.	Vaccine/Batch No.

Date Given ....
Signature

Date Given ....
Signature

....

WEIGHT (LB/KG)

Actual ....   Recommended ....

APPETITE

- ☐ Decreased
- ☐ Normal
- ☐ Increased

DRINKING

- ☐ Decreased
- ☐ Normal
- ☐ Increased

CHECKLIST

- ☐ Eyes
- ☐ Ears
- ☐ Teeth
- ☐ Skin
- ☐ Lungs
- ☐ Heart
- ☐ Abdomen
- ☐ Diet
- ☐ Flea
- ☐ Control
- ☐ Worming
- ☐ Nails

RECOMMENDATIONS

....

....

ID Chip Checked .... Position of ID Chip .... Next Check Due ....

Year _____ health check

Your dog has been vaccinated against

- ☐ Distemper
- ☐ Hepatitis
- ☐ Leptospirosis
- ☐ Parvovirus
- ☐ Parainfluenza
- ☐ Infectious Bronchitis
- ☐ Rabies
- ☐ Other

VACCINATION BOOSTER

Vaccine/Batch No.

Vaccine/Batch No.

Date Given ....
Signature

Date Given ....
Signature

WEIGHT (LB/KG)

Actual ....   Recommended ....

APPETITE

- ☐ Decreased
- ☐ Normal
- ☐ Increased

DRINKING

- ☐ Decreased
- ☐ Normal
- ☐ Increased

CHECKLIST

- ☐ Eyes
- ☐ Abdomen
- ☐ Ears
- ☐ Diet
- ☐ Teeth
- ☐ Flea
- ☐ Skin
- ☐ Control
- ☐ Lungs
- ☐ Worming
- ☐ Heart
- ☐ Nails

RECOMMENDATIONS

....

....

ID Chip Checked .... Position of ID Chip .... Next Check Due ....

Fleas, worms, & ticks

Parasites are not only unpleasant (and itchy), they actually pose a serious risk to my health (and yours), so you must get me treated regularly.

FLEAS Did you know that only about 5% of the flea population around our home are on me; the rest are in the environment? A telltale sign that I have fleas, apart from the fact that I can't stop scratching, is black grit (flea droppings). Left untreated, fleas can cause a serious skin condition called FAD (flea allergy dermatitis). These little creatures also carry tapeworm, so get me treated with year-round protection.

WORMS Worms come in all shapes and sizes, but the most common worms are roundworms, tapeworms, whipworms, and hookworms. Most puppies are born with worms. Untreated they can damage my intestines, and when I poop worm eggs they can lie in the soil and then infect humans, especially children. Worm me once a month until I am 6 months old and then every 3 months after that.

TICKS They suck my blood and spread Lyme disease. Ticks cling on with their jaws, and you might not even notice these tiny pests until they have become engorged (they look a bit like skin tags). Remove with a special plastic tick hook (avoid tweezers, which will squash the tick and encourage it to inject more toxins into my body). Slip the end of the hook underneath the tick and then lift the hook very lightly and TURN IT in an unscrewing action. Don't pull! Check the wound to ensure that the tick's mouth parts have been removed.

Worming record

YEAR 0	Date				
	Product				
YEAR 1	Date				
	Product				
YEAR 2	Date				
	Product				
YEAR 3	Date				
	Product				
YEAR 4	Date				
	Product				
YEAR 5	Date				
	Product				
YEAR 6	Date				
	Product				

Flea control record

	MONTH	JANUARY	FEBRUARY	MARCH	APRIL
YEAR 0	Date				
	Dog				
	House				
YEAR 1	Date				
	Dog				
	House				
YEAR 2	Date				
	Dog				
	House				
YEAR 3	Date				
	Dog				
	House				
YEAR 4	Date				
	Dog				
	House				
YEAR 5	Date				
	Dog				
	House				
YEAR 6	Date				
	Dog				
	House				

MAY	JUNE	JULY	AUGUST	SEPTEMBER	OCTOBER	NOVEMBER	DECEMBER

Bath time!

An old wives' tale says that dogs should only have a bath once a year. However, as long as you use good quality doggie shampoo (human shampoo isn't suitable, because it makes my skin dry) and rinse me thoroughly, there's no reason why you shouldn't bathe me more frequently, especially when I have rolled in something unpleasant (again). If you give me several fun-filled baths while I am still a puppy, then I will learn to love them when I grow up.

If you're going to wash me in the bath, I recommend using a non-slip mat. Brush me thoroughly first to get all the tangles out of my coat, otherwise the water will make them impossible. Use lukewarm water (not too hot!). Wet me all over and use a soothing voice to keep me calm. Avoiding my eyes, work the shampoo into my coat starting at my neck. Rinse thoroughly and then towel dry me quickly before I shake water everywhere.

Place photograph here

Groom me!

All dogs need grooming regularly, not just poodles and long-haired prima donnas. Not only is it good for me (it spreads the natural oils in my coat, making it clean and glossy) but it gives us quality time together and gets me used to be handled. You should be able to groom me everywhere, and I should be able to trust that I'm in safe hands. Choose a time when I am calm (for example, following a walk) and when we won't be interrupted.

My breed should be groomed every ....

Ask a professional groomer for breed-specific information about which tools to use and how to use them.

- Metal comb (for smoothing and removing tangles; for fine or medium-dense coats)
- De-matter (for longer hair and tangles)
- Slicker brush (for the top coat)
- Pin brush (for heavy, medium, fine, or long coats)
- Natural bristle brush
- Rake (for medium dense coats that aren't too long)

Comb in the direction of hair growth, concentrating on small areas at a time. Begin brushing at the head, work down toward the tail and down the legs and flanks.

When grooming me for the first time, give me treats and praise so I link being groomed with pleasure. Start off with short sessions and gradually make them longer when you know I am happy.

Areas I like being groomed (pay special attention)

....

....

....

....

Sensitive places (gently does it)

....

....

....

....

....

Place photograph here

Here I am looking well-groomed and in tiptop condition

Place photograph here

Another photo opportunity!

First aid

No matter how wonderful and careful you are as an owner, accidents and emergencies sometimes happen, especially when I am a puppy.

RESTRAIN ME When I am hurt and distressed I may injure myself by struggling, or try to bite, so you need to keep me restrained. If fear and pain are making me aggressive, muzzle me. Use a length of gauze or a tie. Wrap it twice around my snout, but not too tight, and then tie it around the back of my neck. Make sure I can still breathe easily. Loosen the muzzle slightly if it is inhibiting my breathing.

CANINE CPR We've all seen ER doctors on the TV administering CPR, but I bet you didn't know that you can do it on dogs and save my life. IMPORTANT: ONLY USE CPR IF I HAVE STOPPED BREATHING, OTHERWISE YOU COULD DO ME SERIOUS INJURY. CHECK FOR LIFE SIGNS BEFORE YOU BEGIN.

LIE ME ON MY SIDE. If I'm not breathing, clear my mouth of any obstructions and move my tongue, so that it sticks out of the side of my mouth. Take a deep breath and exhale into my nose. Watch my chest rise as you exhale, which is a sign my lungs are filling. Repeat every ten seconds if I'm a big dog and more frequently if I'm small. After ten breaths do five chest compressions. Place one hand on top of the other over my heart (just behind my front legs); push down five times in short bursts, then return to the breathing. Keep this cycle of ten breaths and five chest compressions going until I start breathing on my own or until the emergency vet arrives.

SHOCK After an accident or injury I may go into shock. My heart beats rapidly, I may be panting and breathing rapidly, or I may be lying with staring dilated pupils. All you can do is keep me warm and get me to the vet as quickly as possible.

HEATSTROKE If you suspect that I have overheated (I have flopped down, won't stop panting, or maybe I'm pacing around in agitation), cover me with a wet towel, hose me down, or dunk me in cold water.

BLEEDING Clean small scrapes and scratches with a clean wet cloth, and while they heal, check them every day to see they haven't become infected. If bleeding is continuous and more serious, place sterile gauze pads on the wound, apply firm pressure, and get me to the vet quickly. If you suspect that I am bleeding internally (I am very restless, I have pale gums, enlarged abdomen, or blood in my stools, saliva, or vomit) rush me to the vet.

CHOKING Open my mouth and try to see what is blocking my airway. Gently remove any obstruction; use a tool (pliers, salad tongs) if you can't reach. If this doesn't work, stand above and behind me, interlock you hands underneath my belly and pull sharply upward three times. If I'm still in trouble, rush me to the vet.

POISONING The common signs of poisoning are extreme salivation, vomiting, diarrhea, and muscle spasms or seizures. Try to discover what I have swallowed, and take a sample of it and me to the vet immediately.

BURNS Put an icepack on the burn (or a pack of frozen peas). If the burn has been caused by chemicals, wash with lots of water (I may also have swallowed some). If my skin is blistered, bleeding, or oozing, get me to the vet quickly. If the skin is merely red, keep it clean and watch out for signs of infection.

Insurance details

Insurance company
....

Address
....
....

Telephone
....

Policy number
....

Details of cover   Maximum   Excess

Vet's fees (injury and illness)
....

Boarding kennel fees
....

Complementary treatment
....

Advertising and reward
....

Third party liability
....

Emergency repatriation (travel)
....

Quarantine expenses and loss of documents
....

Renewal date
....

Premium
....

Choose an insurance company that offers cover
for ongoing care, so that if I need a course of
treatment or have a recurring health problem,
I will still be covered.

CHAPTER 3

Training

All dogs should be trained and that includes me! I may be a cute little puppy now, but I will grow into an unhappy and unruly mutt without proper guidance. In this section I will show you how to be calm and assertive, rather than bossy and noisy, and let you in on a little secret: I will do anything you want me to with the right encouragement. View training as an ongoing process, rather than something you teach me as a puppy and then neglect. Above all, it should be fun!

Principles of training

Training me is about learning how to communicate with and motivate me, rather than bullying me into doing your bidding. If you are prepared to spend some time learning how dogs view the world, then you'll have a much better chance of teaching me the appropriate way to behave, which means that I will be happy and confident. Poorly trained dogs are unhappy and confused.

START TRAINING ME EARLY and continue throughout my life. I will respond to training from about seven weeks old. I recommend two or three sessions a day of between five and ten minutes, and at the end of each session give me lots of praise.

YOU'RE THE BOSS It is important that you show me that you are the leader. I'm a pack animal and I need to know my place in the family, but I don't want to be the leader, because that's a stressful position. I am actually happiest being the lowest in the family hierarchy, so then I don't have the burden of being in charge and fretting every time one of you leaves the house. Keep me below you at all times, and don't let me jump on you or the furniture. Also, pretend to eat a little of my food before you give the bowl to me; dominant members of the pack always eat first.

NEVER HIT ME This will only confuse me and teach me to be frightened of you. Keep calm, project confidence, and show consistency and I will fall into line. Give me lots of attention, but on your terms. For instance, if you want me to stop barking every time someone puts on their shoes, ignore me until I stop and then give me lots of praise. I'll soon learn that pointless, incessant barking doesn't get me anything nice!

DON'T SHOUT OR SCREAM

(I call this verbal smacking). Praise me with a high-pitched voice (and a bit of baby talk, which I love), and correct me with a deep voice.

REWARDS

Praise me for behaving well (and give me treats, though not every time, otherwise I might refuse to do anything unless I get a treat!), and ignore or correct me when I am behaving badly. You must respond within one second or else I will think you are rewarding me and correcting me for something else. For example, don't bother scolding me for peeing on the floor while you're out, because I won't understand why I am being punished.

BE CONSISTENT

Write down the house rules (see pages 60–61) and make sure that everyone sticks to them (that's me and my canine friends, I mean). If I am not allowed on the furniture, there should be no exceptions. When training, always use the same key words and hand gestures for each command. However, you should vary the distance at which you give me commands.

GIVE A SIGNAL ONCE

If you're trying to get me to sit and you say it five times and I sit on the fifth time, you teach me to sit on the fifth time! Give me one verbal and physical cue, and if I don't respond I don't get a reward.

NO DISTRACTIONS

When you train me, train me in places free from distractions like noise or other dogs. Once my training is solid you can introduce distractions to deepen my focus and concentration.

HAVE FUN

If you don't make training fun for both of us, then it will become a big chore. Sure, you'll need time and patience, but the end result is well worth the effort.

I can sit!

Get my attention by calling my name. When I bound over to you, hold a treat between your finger and thumb and let me sniff it, but don't let me eat it (don't say anything yet). Eventually I will probably sit down. Immediately give me the treat and lots of praise. Repeat this a few more times and then introduce the verbal and physical cues. As I sit say sit and raise your wrist slightly, then give me the treat. Repeat this ten times. Finally, ask me to sit before I start to sit and repeat this ten times.

Place passport size photograph here

If I don't respond, withdraw the treat.

52

I can lie down!

Ask me to sit. Holding a treat, place the same hand flat on the floor in front of me. Let me sniff the treat. When I eventually lie down on my belly (while I work out how to get it), give me the treat and lots of praise. Repeat this a few more times and then introduce the verbal and physical cues. As you bring your hand down say **down**. Repeat ten times.

Place photograph here

I can stay!

Ask me to sit and then stand in front of me. Place your palm in front of my face and say, **stay** (in this case it is OK to repeat the instruction if necessary as stay is a continuous action). After a second give me a treat. Repeat several times, leaving an increasingly longer gap between the command and the treat, until I am able to stay for ten seconds consistently. Now it is time to increase the distance: take a step back and give me the stay command. Gradually increase the distance until I can stay even when you are several yards away. Walk back to me to give me the treat (rather than let me run to you, otherwise you are rewarding me for not staying!).

Place photograph here

I can stand!

When I stand up from a lying or sitting position, give me lots of praise and a treat. Repeat a few times and then as I stand up add the verbal command **stand** and a gesture: raise your arm from the elbow with palm facing upward. Repeat five times, then give the command before I stand.

Place photograph here

I can come!

It is really important to teach me this command, because nothing is more frustrating for you than waiting for me to finish having fun before wandering back to you in my own time.

Teach me that **come** needn't always mean the end of my fun, by calling me to come, rewarding me with a really special treat (chicken anyone?), and then letting me go play again. Then, when you call me to put me on the leash, I will expect something nice to happen.

If I don't come immediately, start walking or running away in the direction you want me to go. I love playing chase, so I will usually follow.

If I don't come immediately, don't get angry with me, otherwise I will associate coming back to you with getting yelled at, and will be less likely to come on command. When I come, no matter how long I have taken, give me lots of praise. When you're taking me for a walk carry treats, so you can reward me for coming to you.

Place passport size photograph here

I can leave it!

This is another important command, because there will be times when it is super important that I leave something alone (for example, something that might harm me or make me harm others). The trick is to give me a good reason not to satisfy my hunger or curiosity.

Place a treat in your closed hand with a little piece left sticking out. Let me sniff it. As soon as I move my head away from the treat, praise me and then let me have the treat. Repeat this a few times and then add the command **leave it**. Repeat several times and then extend the challenge by rewarding me with a treat from your other hand rather than the one I am supposed to leave. Next, leave a treat on the floor. When I show an interest say, **leave it**. If I turn my head away or look at you, give me the treat from your other hand, and lots of praise. Finally, replace the floor treat with other objects that you want me to leave, and repeat.

Place photograph here

I can walk on a leash!

Teaching me to walk on a leash is important for my and your safety. Pulling can damage my throat, not to mention your arm (and dignity). Teach me this skill while I am young rather than after I have grown so big that I can pull you across a busy road!

If I pull on the leash don't pull back, just stand still and remain calm. When I stop pulling, give me lots of praise and begin walking again. This way I will soon learn that if I want to get somewhere fast, straining on my leash will actually get me there slower.

Place passport size photograph here

I can heel!

Once I am walking well on a leash, you can teach me to heel on the leash and then off the leash. Don't use this command all the time, just when you need me to be close by (for example, in a crowded street).

Walk normally, and when I just happen to walk next to you (with my shoulders level with your thigh), give me lots of praise and a reward. Repeat a few times, then the next time it happens pat your thigh and say, **heel** followed by praise and a treat. Soon I will associate heel with treats, and I will be eager to do it whenever you give the command.

Place photograph here

House rules

It is important that you establish house rules as soon as I arrive, and make sure that everyone in the household knows and sticks to them, otherwise I am going to get mighty confused.

Things I am allowed to do

....

....

....

....

....

....

....

....

....

....

Things I am not allowed to do

....

....

....

....

....

....

....

....

....

....

....

....

Place photograph here

I am sooo well trained!

CHAPTER 4

MAKING
friends

As I grow and find my way in the world, I will experience lots of new sights, sounds, smells, people, and animals. It is your job to introduce me to all this in such a way that I increase my confidence and conquer my fears. This process is called socialization.

Socialization

Socialization is an important part of my development (that's a fancy way of saying that I need help learning how to live in the world), and while it starts at home with you, it is vital that early on you introduce me to life beyond your four walls. Every day I should meet new challenges and things I have never seen before. Some of them will scare me, so it's important that you help me to overcome my fears.

BEING HANDLED Dogs love to be stroked and petted, but we have to learn to be comfortable with it. It's not something we're born with. Like a human baby, I like exploring the world with my mouth (only I don't grow out of it), so when I am a puppy, when you stroke me, I am likely to try to play bite your hands. Don't let me, even for fun. Give a little yelp to tell me biting is unacceptable. Give me toys to chew and play tug-of-war games with them, but don't let me grow up believing that it's OK to chew people.

WEEKS EIGHT TO TWELVE

Socialization continues throughout puppyhood, but weeks eight to 12 are crucial. After 16 weeks puppies greet their world with much greater caution, and during the eighth week we go through a fear period where we are super-cautious about everything, so don't expose me to anything scary during this week. If something does scare me, don't give me lots of cuddles and soothing talk, because this rewards me for being frightened. Instead, try to distract me with a toy or a pat; make me think about something else and move on without turning the incident into a big deal.

If I start barking at something, such as the laundry on the clothes line, a creaking gate, or a tree in the yard, take me with you to explore this new and alarming object. Talk soothingly, let me sniff it and learn that clothes, creaks, and trees can do me no harm! Give me lots of praise and rewards when I conquer my fear.

BUILD CONFIDENCE The more positive experiences you can give me in those early weeks (as well as the first two years of my life), the more confidently I will face new challenges as an adult. Make sure I meet lots of new people and dogs (so long as they are healthy, vaccinated, and well-behaved; and that goes for the dogs, too!).

Take me for short, frequent trips in the car and give me lots of treats. Stop the car and let me watch the world go by through the window. I will soon think the car is a fun place to be.

Take me to the vet just to say hi, and give me some more treats. Don't wait until I need a jab or feel poorly.

Don't force or rush me into new experiences. Let me go at my own pace, and don't reward me for being fearful. Distract me and give me treats and cuddles when I am behaving appropriately.

INDEPENDENCE I am completely dependent on you for my welfare, but that doesn't mean that I should follow you everywhere and rely on you totally for my emotional security. In fact, don't let me. Close the door and teach me that it's OK to be on my own sometimes; and don't always respond to my demands for attention. When you leave me in the house on my own, don't make a big deal of it, and don't make a fuss when you return. Show me that you come and go, but you always come back before long. Try not to leave me for more than half an hour at first, and when I am older, no longer than six hours.

Socialization does not end in puppyhood. You must lay the foundations during my first few months, but also reinforce social skills throughout my life.

How to make doggy friends

Once I have had my vaccinations, introduce me to lots of other dogs of all different shapes, sizes, ages, breeds, and temperament.

It is vital that you don't reinforce negative associations by your own anxiety or tension. If I show aggression toward another dog while I am walking on the leash and you tighten the leash and shout at me, I will soon associate meeting strange dogs with anxiety, and this will make me even more aggressive. Don't punish me for growling or barking at other dogs. Try to distract my attention and give me a treat as soon as I stop showing aggression, so that next time I meet another dog we can both anticipate a good outcome.

Make a record of the dogs I meet regularly on my walks, and use this list to spot common patterns or situations and to plan how to resolve potential problems.

Dogs I meet on my walks

....

....

My reactions

....

....

....

....

....

....

....

....

....

....

Place photograph
of me with other dogs here

Puppy party!

A puppy party is an informal get-together for puppies and their owners and is a fun way to encourage me to mix with both dogs and people. They are usually held at the vet's office, and a nurse should be present to answer your questions. But why not throw a few puppy parties at home!

- Make sure that everyone on the guest list is free of diseases and parasites and has had their first vaccination.
- Invite all kinds of dogs and people, especially men (scary deep voices) and children (hyperactive), as both these types of human can frighten puppies at first.
- Ask your guests to leave their shoes outside and wash their hands before handling me.
- Everyone should bring some toys and lots of treats and encourage your guests to play with me, hand-feed me, and even give me a few commands and lots of cuddles and physical contact. This will help me quickly learn that meeting new people and dogs is an exciting and treat-filled wonderland!
- Don't worry if I take part in a little play fighting with other dogs: it's the best way for me to learn boundaries and to mouth gently.

Place photograph here

Here I am at my first puppy party

My playmates

I have made lots of new friends!

Place passport size photographs here

Place passport size photographs here

Place passport size photographs here

Place passport size photographs here

Place passport size photographs here

70

CHAPTER 5

HAVING *fun*

What's the point of having me if we're not going
to have lots of fun together! Play is one of the best
ways to bond and provides the structure that helps us
better communicate, as well as helping to keep me fit and
mentally active. If you're stuck for ideas, this section
should kick-start your sense of adventure.

Games & tricks

I love playing games; and if I don't get a good play session in several times a week I'll get bored. It's a great way to teach me some good lessons. Good games teach me that you are in charge and that you are kind and fair. Bad games teach me that I am stronger and faster than you!

PLAY BOW When I lie my front legs down and stick my bum in air, tail wagging, I am saying, **play with me!** Also I might bring you a toy or nudge you with my nose or a paw.

RETRIEVING GAMES Some dogs are natural retrievers, but most of us can be taught to enjoy fetching stuff. When teaching me to retrieve begin by rolling a ball across the floor, so that I can visually follow it. If you simply hurl an object into the stratosphere and then yell **fetch**, how on earth am I supposed to know what's expected of me? Start with little steps and build up, and when I bring something back, really praise me. If I won't drop it, then gently press my upper lips against my upper teeth and say, **drop it** and then give me lots of praise when I do.

HIDE-AND-SEEK GAMES This teaches me to show off my nasal super powers. This is best played with two humans. One of you hides (not too far away at first), then the other one says, **go find (their name).** Off I trot, sniffing the ground to follow their scent, and when I find them, they give me some treats. What's not to like about that! As I get more skilled, hide farther away and take the game outside. You can also hide treats around the house and make me seek them out.

THREE CUPS This is an extension of hide-and-seek. Place a treat under one of three upturned cups and shuffle them around. Get me to sniff out where the treat is hiding. Eventually you'll be able to teach me to indicate which one with my paw!

THE NAME GAME Send me to fetch a tennis ball a few times, with the instruction **(my name), get the tennis ball**. Then put it away and send me to fetch a chew toy a few times: **(my name), get the chew toy!** Next, place both objects on the floor and tell me to fetch one of them. Give me lots of praise when I succeed and stay silent when I don't (no scolding, please!). You'll be amazed just how many names I can learn!

GAMES TO AVOID Don't play games with me that show me how much stronger or faster I am than you. If you must play tug-of-war, then be sure to win most of the time, otherwise I will start to doubt your leadership abilities. If you want to stop the game, don't just walk away (admitting defeat). Tell me to **drop it!** and give me lots of praise when I obey. Whatever game we play, always consider what it is teaching me.

I CAN GIVE YOU MY PAW Say, **give me your paw** and gently place my paw in your hand. Then give me lots of praise. Repeat this several times, until I am comfortable with this. Then say, **give me your paw**, wait a couple of seconds, then place my paw in your hand and give me lots of praise. Keep repeating and eventually I will place my paw into your hand. Give me lots of praise and a treat and keep practicing.

I CAN ROLL OVER (this one is easy to learn in three stages)
1. Ask me to **sit** and then give me the **lie down** command. Then crouch down beside me, circle a treat over my nose, and I will naturally roll over to try to reach it. Repeat several times.
2. Add the command **roll over** as I roll, then praise me and give me the treat. Repeat several times.
3. Finally, give just the verbal command without circling the treat. Give me the treat after I roll over.

Times when I am naughty!

Place photograph here

Times when I am cute!

....
....
....
....
....
....
....
....
....
....
....

20 things all dogs should do in their lifetime

Have I done any of these yet? Check them off when I do.

- Destroy a brand new pair of slippers
- Play in the sea
- Demolish sand castles on the beach
- Chase a rabbit
- Enter a pet-show costume competition
- Roll in horse or cow muck
- Catch the mail person
- Romp in the snow
- Go jogging in the spring air
- Howl at the moon
- Have a massage
- Burst a heap of balloons
- Ride a skate board
- Eat a banana smeared with peanut butter
- Eat a smaller dog (only kidding!)
- Scatter a pile of freshly raked leaves
- Climb a mountain
- Watch a sunset
- Play ball
- Sneak a pork chop

Place photograph here

Movie star mutt

Paws up all those who remember Rin Tin Tin. If you dream of turning me into a screen or pin-up legend in my own back yard, then check out this master class in mutt-based photo taking and movie making.

If you want me to look my best on the silver screen, then follow these tips:

• Close ups show my personality: it's all in the eyes. Forget about long shots; get in real close and make sure you make the most of my peepers (they're my best feature). If you film me from behind and you can't see my eyes, it does nothing for me, and the shot or take will have a "so what" quality you want to avoid. If your photos or movies are dull, get in even closer.

• Shoot from a low angle, preferably on my eye level, for maximum interaction. You may even have to lie on the ground for the best results. When you shoot me from above, you lose the magic of interaction and the result is bo-oring. I'm yawning already, and so will your audience.

• Get the light right. You don't need to be a lighting designer to know that natural light is best, but that dappled lighting indoors can also be real interesting too. If you need to use a flash, angle it away from me or I'll be all washed out.

• Avoid snapping me in the middle of the frame. It's more interesting if I'm off to the side (and make sure the background contrasts with my fur).

• If you're filming a movie, try to tell a story, no matter how basic it is.

• For movies, switch angles often. Don't film from one angle for longer than ten seconds; and when you zoom in and out do it to a count of five.

Place photograph here

Place photograph here

Here's me in Spring

Place photograph here

Here's me in Summer

Place photograph here

Here's me in Fall

Place photograph here

Here's me in Winter

Homemade gourmet treats

Why buy gourmet doggy treats when you can make your own? Or rather, what I meant to say was to keep buying all the doggy treats and then make even more at home.

PEANUT BUTTER AND MEAL TREATS
YOU'LL NEED:
2 cups (300 g) whole wheat flour
$\frac{1}{2}$ cup (65 g) corn meal
2 teaspoons bone meal
2 tablespoons vegetable oil
$\frac{1}{2}$ cup (140 g) smooth peanut butter
2 large eggs mixed with a $\frac{1}{4}$ cup (60 ml) beef stock
1 teaspoon iodized salt

Mix all the dry ingredients in a large bowl. Make a well in the middle and pour in the peanut butter, oil, and egg stock, and stir to combine. Knead the dough on a floured board for three minutes, adding additional stock if the dough is too dry or stiff. Let the dough sit in a warm place for half an hour.

Roll the dough to about $^1/_2$ inch (1 cm) thickness, cut into shapes with a cookie cutter, then space them 1 inch (2.5 cm) apart on a greased baking sheet. Bake in a preheated oven 350°F (180°C) for approximately 30 minutes or until golden brown. Turn off the oven and allow the treats to crisp up overnight, then store in an airtight container.

LIVER TREATS

YOU'LL NEED:

1 lb (16 oz) raw liver

1 egg

$1^1/_2$ cups (225 g) whole wheat flour

$^1/_4$ teaspoon brewers' yeast

$^1/_4$ teaspoon oregano

Blend the liver into a paste and mix well with the other ingredients in a large bowl, then follow the instructions above and bake for 30 minutes for chewy treats; longer for crisper treats.

Place photograph here

Me playing my favorite game

CHAPTER 6

In Safe
HANDS

Even though we are joined at the hip,
there will be times when you need to get someone
else to look after me for a few days. It is
important that they know all about me and my
daily requirements, so be sure to make lots of
notes in this section so they won't go barking
up the wrong tree.

Dog Sitters

NAME
....
phone
....
email
....
rates
....
NAME
....
phone
....
email
....
rates
....
NAME
....
phone
....
email
....
rates
....
NAME
....
phone
....
email
....
rates
....

Notes for the dog sitter

Feeding

....

....

....

Walking

....

....

Additional notes

....

....

....

Phone

Backup contact

Vet

Dog walkers

NAME
....
phone
....
email
....
rates
....
NAME
....
phone
....
email
....
rates
....

....

Dog kennels

Contact details
....

....
Phone
....
Daily rate
....
Special requirements
....
Notes
....

Useful addresses & numbers

Notes

Notes

Notes

Notes

Notes